SONS:
A FATHER'S LOVE

SONS:
A FATHER'S
LOVE

*Heart-lifting
stories of
dads and their boys*

Bob Carlisle

WORD PUBLISHING
NASHVILLE
A Thomas Nelson Company

BOB CARLISLE
BUTTERFLY KISSES

Published by Word Publishing, Nashville, Tennessee

© 1999 Bob Carlisle

Lyrics written by Bob Carlisle and Randy Thomas. © 1998 Diadem Music Publishing/SESAC (A division of Brentwood-Benson Music Publishing, Inc.) Damascus Road Music/ASCAP

Library of Congress Cataloging-in-Publication Data

Carlisle, Bob, 1956–
Sons : a father's love / by Bob Carlisle.
p.   cm.
ISBN 08499-1611-9
1. Fathers and sons Anecdotes. I. Title.
HQ755.85.C3577   1999
306.874'2—dc21

Printed in the United States of America
9 0 1 2 3 4 5 6 BVG 9 8 7 6 5 4 3 2 1

Dear Reader,

The song "Butterfly Kisses" was a big success in the record business, and it drew a lot of attention to the invaluable relationship that binds together the hearts of fathers and their daughters. I think it reminded people that dads play a unique role in the lives of their children—a role that is both integral and irreplaceable. Since that record was released, countless people have asked if I was going to write a similar song about fathers and sons.

As every songwriter knows, songs are like children in that each is unique. Just as "Butterfly Kisses" was written for my daughter, Brooke, to convey my feelings about watching her grow up, the song "A Father's Love" was written for my son, Evan, to impart to him the knowledge that he is deeply and unconditionally loved. That fact, I am convinced, will help make him strong as he grows up to be a man himself.

I know "A Father's Love" has touched the hearts of countless men and boys, because I have

v

been hearing from them. Some of the stories they've told me are collected for you to read in the following pages.

Sometimes the stories were told to me in person, and sometimes they were written in letters or posted on our Web site, www.bobcarlisle.com. I am also very grateful to the National Center for Fathering in Kansas City, Missouri, for sharing some of the letters they have received from sons who wrote about their fathers.

Like the stories we published in *Butterfly Kisses and Bittersweet Tears*, these stories don't all have happy endings and they aren't all about perfect fathers. I believe in the power of "real stories"—because if we listen carefully we will recognize something true that might also pertain to ourselves. The names of the writers are protected to guard their privacy.

Butterfly Kisses and Bittersweet Tears meant so much to so many; I suspect you'll enjoy reading these stories, too. As the song says, "There is no power on earth like your father's love." The compelling message that comes through every father-and-son story is that dads play a more important role in their sons' lives than we ever imagined. As you read, you'll discover, as I did, that the love between a father and a son deeply affects their lives, and it also mirrors the love of our heavenly Father. I am convinced that the reflection of that powerful mystery can be glimpsed in these individual stories.

Bob Carlisle

FATHER'S LOVE

BY BOB CARLISLE AND RANDY THOMAS

There feet tall, and full of questions
You must have thought I was the smartest man alive
I didn't always have the answers
To every little how and where and why
Like *Daddy, why's the sky so blue today?*
Does Jesus really hear me when I pray?
When I grow up, will I be just like you?
Will I be tall and strong and brave?

CHORUS:
There is no power on earth like your father's love
So big and so strong as your father's love
A promise that's sacred, a promise from heaven above
No matter where you go . . . always know
You can depend on your father's love.

Especially when it's cold, especially when you're lonely

When your little heart is just trying to find its way

I know the world is always changing

But just remember, son, that some things never change

So even when my time on earth is through

There still will be a part of me in you

'Cause some things are forever

Nothing's ever gonna take my love from you

SECOND CHORUS:

There is no power on earth like your father's love

So big and so strong as your father's love

A promise that's sacred, a promise from heaven above

Did I hug enough? Did I care enough?

When you most needed me, was I there enough?

Enough to make you feel the power of your father's love?

Sons:
A Father's Love

PART ONE

There is no power on earth like your father's love

So big and so strong as your father's love . . .

Most of us receive our sons as newborn babies, and our hearts swell with love for them the minute they are placed in our arms. Other men step into ready-made families and ably fill the shoes of a dad, even when their sons aren't "flesh and blood." Still others choose to stand in the gap that remains when a father has gone away and left his job undone. These may be grandfathers, friends, teachers, or good, generous men with a heart for kids—men who see a need and choose to meet it.

The fatherly love that a man extends toward a young boy is, indeed, like no other power on earth. It is not only big and strong, it is life-giving and life-changing. It blesses both the father (or father figure) and the son. Most of all, it is one of God's richest gifts to our world.

My father loved cars. He tuned them up, rubbed them down, and knew every sound and smell and idiosyncrasy of every car he owned. He was also very picky about who drove his cars. So when I got my driver's license at sixteen, I was a little worried about the responsibility of leaving home in one of his beloved vehicles. He had a beautiful red Chevy pickup, a big white Suburban, and a Mustang convertible with a hot V-8 engine. Every one of them was in prime condition. He also had a short temper and very little patience with carelessness, especially if his kids happened to be the careless ones.

One afternoon he sent me to town in the Chevy truck with the assignment of bringing back a list of things he needed for some odd jobs around the house. It hadn't been long since I'd gotten my license, so it was still a novelty to be seen driving around, and Dad's red pickup was a good truck to be seen in. I carefully maneuvered my way toward downtown, watching carefully at each light, trying to drive as defensively as he'd always told me to do. The thought of a collision in one of Dad's cars was enough to make me the safest driver in town. I didn't even want to think about it.

I was heading through a green light and was in the middle of a main downtown intersection when an elderly man, who somehow hadn't seen the red light, plowed into the passenger side of the Chevy. I slammed on the brakes, hit a slick spot in the road, and spun into a curb; the pickup rolled over onto its side.

I was dazed at first, and my face was bleeding from a couple of glass cuts, but the seat belt had kept me from serious injury. I was vaguely concerned about the danger of fire, but the engine had died, and before long I heard the sound of sirens. I had just begun to wonder how much longer I'd be trapped inside when a couple of firemen helped me get out, and soon I was sitting on the curb, my aching head in my hands, my face and shirt dripping with blood.

That's when I got a good look at Dad's red pickup. It was scraped and dented and crushed, and I was surprised that I had walked away from it in one piece. And by then I was sort of wishing I hadn't, because it suddenly dawned on me that I would soon have to face Dad with some very bad news about one of his pride-and-joy cars.

We lived in a small town, and several people who saw the accident knew me. Someone must have called Dad right away, because it wasn't long after I was rescued from the wreck that he came running up to me. I closed my eyes, not wanting to see his face.

"Dad, I'm so sorry—"

"Terry, are you all right?" Dad's voice didn't sound at all like I thought it would. When I looked up, he was on his knees next to me on the curb, his hands gently lifting my cut face and studying my wounds. "Are you in a lot of pain?"

"I'm okay. I'm really sorry about your truck."

"Forget the truck, Terry. The truck's a piece of machinery. I'm concerned about you, not the truck. Can you get up? Can you walk? I'll drive you to the hospital unless you think you need an ambulance."

I shook my head. "I don't need an ambulance. I'm fine."

Dad carefully put his hands under my arms and lifted me to my feet. I looked up at him uncertainly and was amazed to see that his face was a study in compassion and concern. "Can you make it?" he asked, and his voice sounded scared.

"I'm fine, Dad. Really. Why don't we just go home? I don't need to go to the hospital."

We compromised and went to the family doctor, who cleaned up my wounds, bandaged me, and sent me on my way. I don't recall when the truck got towed, how long I was laid up, or what I did for the rest of that night. All I know is that for the first time in my life, I understood that my father loved me. I hadn't realized it before, but Dad loved me more than his truck, more than any of his cars, more than I could have possibly imagined.

Since that day we've had our ups and downs,

and I've disappointed him enough to make him mad, but one thing remains unchanging. Dad loved me then, he loves me now, and he'll love me for the rest of my life.

T.J.

I think the best part of being a dad is that it gives me an excuse to have fun. I get more pleasure out of being with my boys than I do from anything else in the world. And, since spending quality time with them is something dads are supposed to do, I can actually do what I like best and still be acting responsibly!

At 4:30 on Saturday mornings, I wake Kevin and Jeremy up and we all pile into the car and head for the lake. We fish all day, talk, and relax. It seems like all my worries are a million miles away when we're bobbing around in our little boat, watching the water and the clouds, and enjoying each other's company.

Sundays we all go to church together—my wife, our daughters, and the boys. That evening we read stories to each other out loud. With our imaginations, we turn our living room into a bug-infested jungle, a dangerous spy's headquarters, or a peaceful seaside village. We all read in voices that fit the characters, and everyone loves it.

During the week, Kevin and I wash the dog, and I try to help Jeremy improve his pitching arm. Since the boys are so different, I have to make equal time for each of them. If I don't get too carried away with one or the other, there is rarely any competition between them. Of course the girls want to spend time with Dad, too, so it keeps me busy.

The most fun of all for me comes at holiday times. My boys and I are the Christmas decorators, the Easter bread bakers, and the Fourth of July fireworks team. We love nothing better than getting everything ready for the girls to see, and they are always surprised and delighted.

I guess in some ways our family is a little old-fashioned. We don't watch much television, and we haven't got a lot of money to spend. But I never had a dad to spend time with me, and I want to make the most of the years I have with my kids. Most of all, I want to be a good male role model for my sons, because they've got to face a lot of hard decisions in the future and maybe the time I spend with them will help them be wise and prepared for whatever they decide to do.

For me, the best thing about being a dad is that when I'm doing the most important thing I could possibly do, I'm also doing the thing I enjoy the most.

N.C.

If all dads were like my dad, the world would be perfect. You wouldn't hear anyone complaining about a bad childhood; you wouldn't hear anyone saying that their father didn't have time for them or didn't love them. You would hear kids talking about how great their dads are. If all dads were like my dad, the world would be full of good role models and fathers who love their children.

I admire my dad more than anyone else I know. He's not rich. He's not a pro athlete. He's not famous. None of these things matters because my dad is everything important to me. In my eyes the perfect father should love his family, do what is right, put his family before his job, and most of all, love God. My dad fits this description perfectly.

One reason I admire my father is that he pursues his dreams. At one time my dad had a well-paying job as a district manager for a sporting goods company. He gave all of this up to pursue his lifelong dream of becoming a doctor and following God's will. It's not easy to become a doctor. The minimum amount of training is eleven years! He's in his eighth year. This shows that he's also willing to sacrifice—just like all good fathers should.

My dad has always been there for me. Whenever I need help or advice, he is who I go to. We have gone through the good and bad times together. I love him and he loves me. It's not like any other love. It's a deep love that could go through anything. My relationship with my dad is worth more than anything else in the world. I just wish that every kid could say the same.

S.A.—AGE 13

About a decade ago, when I had about fifty pounds more hair and fifty pounds less me, I was the lead singer of the Christian rock band Allies. Our band was very energetic and quite adept at performing for large festival audiences. This had never gone unnoticed by two-year-old Evan. With his bright gold-colored toy guitar, he took great pleasure in emulating his dad onstage.

One night at a Christian rock festival in southern California, Allies had taken the stage. We were having a great time and the audience was revved up to a fever pitch. At the side, just off-stage, were my wife, Jacque, and a very excited toddler named Evan. And around Evan's neck, slung low in great rock 'n roll fashion, was his gold toy guitar. He was showing his best moves. He was ready. He was so cute that two members of our crew stood him on top of a large rolling road case and wheeled him out onto the stage—during the middle of a song, no less.

The audience went wild. So did Evan. The louder the audience cheered, the more intense his moves became. He was the undisputed hit of the evening.

B.C.

When I was sixteen and finally had my own car, Dad told me to be in by 12:30. I didn't mind having a curfew—every kid I knew had to be in by a certain time. But when I turned eighteen, I guess I kind of rebelled at the idea. I didn't really feel like talking to Dad about it because I didn't want to argue with him. But one night I stayed over at my friend's house until 2:00 A.M.

When I finally rolled into our driveway, I noticed that the lights were still on in the living room. I tiptoed through the door, but my efforts not to disturb anyone were wasted: Mom and Dad were sitting on the couch together, and Mom was crying.

"What are you guys doing up?" I asked innocently.

"Waiting for you to come home," my father said in a calm voice. "We figured something had happened to you, because you always call if you're going to be late. Are you all right?"

"Of course I'm all right," I retorted defensively. "I'm eighteen years old and I shouldn't have to check in with you like a child. I don't need rules like that, Dad."

"It's not about rule keeping, David. It's about consideration. The only reason we want you to call us is to keep us from worrying. We really thought something had happened to you tonight."

"Yeah, right . . . well I'm fine. And I'm here, so let's all go to bed." My voice sounded colder than I meant for it to. "Sorry for the inconvenience . . . ," I added, sounding a little too formal for the occasion.

Two weeks later, my folks went out somewhere. They may have told me where they were going, but I wasn't really listening. At midnight, I realized that they weren't home yet. I was working on my car, and I didn't think much about it until 1:00. Then I started wondering where they were. By 1:30 I was feeling uneasy. By 2:00 I was really worried. And by 2:45, I was trying to figure out whether to call the highway patrol or not. I decided to make the call. My hands shook as I picked up the phone, and just as I pushed the 9 in 911, I heard Dad's car pull into the driveway.

Moments later they walked through the door, all dressed up and looking very happy.

"Where have you been?" I roared. "I was just calling the police when you pulled up."

"Why on earth were you calling the police? We were in the city at a play. I told you where we were going."

"You didn't tell me anything! You should have let me know . . ."

Mom looked sympathetic, but Dad didn't.

"I thought you'd had a wreck or something," I continued, gradually realizing that the tables had been turned.

Dad's face was serious, but he had a telltale twinkle in his eye. "We can come home any time we want," he countered, looking me in the eye.

"Of course you can, but . . ."

"Now do you understand why it's a good idea to let people know where you are?" Dad squeezed my shoulder. "It's not about curfews, it's about consideration."

I felt something wet on my face and realized that my eyes were overflowing with tears. Only then did I understand how scared I had been and just how thoroughly I had learned my lesson.

D.B.

When I was a child, my family life was a war zone. My parents drank fairly heavily from time to time, and even when they weren't drinking, they fought about everything. Why they stayed together I'll never know. Maybe they loved one another in some strange way. Maybe they thought divorce was worse than fighting. Or maybe they just liked torturing each other.

Throughout my boyhood one of their biggest arguments centered on whether or not Dad was my real father. Unlike the typical situation where the mom tries to convince her husband that a child is his, in this case my mother swore that I wasn't my father's son. She also made a point, whenever she got the chance, of letting him know that it was none of his business who my father really was!

Despite his drinking bouts and his anger, I really admired my father and secretly wanted to be like him. He was a successful doctor in our small town, and everyone loved him. I was proud to be known as his son and wanted desperately to believe that I was truly his.

At times, when he wasn't looking, I would study Dad's face, searching for a resemblance to mine. Once I found some photographs of him as a boy, and I couldn't help but think we looked exactly the same. And beyond any physical resemblance, I also noticed that we always seemed to understand each other. We had a kind of silent way of communicating, where our eyes would meet and we would smile in some sort of mutual agreement. I believed most of the time that Dad loved me. But still the doubts lingered—was he my father or wasn't he?

The subject was only raised in the heat of battle—and even then, it was my mother's choice weapon, only used when all other defenses seemed to be failing. It worked very well, never failing to enrage Dad. I don't think she ever knew that it wounded me as deeply as it infuriated him. I'm not sure she even remembered those drunken arguments once they were over. But I know Dad did.

One day Dad and I were walking through our town together. I was in my teens by then and had already grown as tall as he was. It was a cold day, with snowflakes drifting in the air, and we were both bundled up in heavy overcoats, gloves, and neck scarves. We turned a corner and simultaneously caught a glimpse of our reflection in a store window as we walked toward it. The two men we saw were the same size. They walked the same way. Each had one hand in a pocket and the other at his side. They had the same angle of posture. Their heads were tilted the same way. And their facial expressions, at first glance, were the same. Dad and I looked like identical twins.

We both laughed out loud. Dad patted my shoulder, a warm, happy smile on his face. "Like father, like son," he said, still chuckling.

We never talked about it again, but from that day on, Dad and I both knew that he was my father. The next time Mom raised the issue, he just laughed at her. And to my knowledge, she never mentioned it again.

N.S.

My parents adopted me when I was just a baby, and they were so happy to have me. They always told me the story about going to the hospital and seeing me for the first time. It was the biggest day in their lives, and that made me feel really special. Dad was a quiet man, and he wasn't really comfortable saying loving words and showing a lot of affection. His quietness sometimes made me uneasy, but I knew that he loved me just as if I were his own flesh and blood.

When I was about six, I begged and pleaded for a puppy. Dad didn't like dogs very much—he thought they were more trouble than they were worth. But, outvoted by Mom and me, eventually he gave in. One Saturday, Mom found an ad in the paper for free puppies, and Dad took me to get one.

Of course I fell in love with her immediately. I named her Rosie, and young as I was, I took very good care of her. I even house-trained her myself, and she always did what I told her to do. Dad hadn't really wanted a dog, but when he saw how responsible I had become, he seemed satisfied that Rosie wasn't so bad after all.

After about six months, a visiting neighbor left our front door open by accident when she went home. And while Mom and I were eating lunch, Rosie ran out the door and disappeared. We didn't notice she was gone for a couple of hours, and by then we had no idea which direction she'd headed. I was devastated. I kept pleading to go look for Rosie, but Mom couldn't leave my baby brother to go out searching and she wouldn't let me go alone.

When Dad got home, I was afraid that he'd be glad Rosie was gone or that he would be upset with me for not taking proper care of her. But I was wrong. He put his hand on my shoulder and said, "After supper we'll go find her."

It was still light when we started out. First we walked up and down every street in the neighborhood. Then we drove to some more outlying areas. At one point, we saw a furry mound in the middle of the road that could have been a dead or injured dog. "Don't look," Dad said. He got out and examined the animal. "It wasn't Rosie," he said, smiling. "It was a raccoon."

Dad was tired from a long day at work, and he must have longed to stretch out in front of the television as he often did. But he spent every minute of the evening looking for Rosie with me. Finally, at about 10:30, we headed home. I was pretty sure he was as disappointed as I was.

I started to get out of the car, but he asked me to wait a minute. "I think I'd like to pray for Rosie," he told me. I was really surprised. Although our family had often prayed about people and problems, I never thought Dad would pray about a lost dog. But he did.

We walked into the house and Mom was waiting for us, an excited look on her face. "A lady called. I think she has Rosie."

Tired as he was, Dad got the address and headed back to the car. I trotted after him, hoping the lady had the right "mutt," as she had described the dog she'd found. Sure enough, it was Rosie. Dad picked her up, gently rubbed her ears, and checked her over for injuries. Then, without a word, he handed her to me and headed for the house.

"It's almost bedtime," he remarked as we walked into the house. "Thank God Rosie's home. You'll sleep better knowing she's all right. For that matter, so will I."

E.S.

My father died in an automobile accident when I was two years old, and I don't remember him at all. After the accident, my mother moved back in with her parents, and I guess you'd say that from that time on, my grandfather really became my dad. He did so much for me that I can't possibly remember everything. But more than that, he and I really understood each other.

At first I was kind of a scared little boy, and it didn't take much to frighten me. Grandpa never once criticized me or made fun of me. Instead, he would listen carefully to me and then talk to me about my fears. At night, when I was afraid of the dark, he would sit on the side of my bed until I fell asleep. Sometimes he told me bedtime stories about Big Foot, but he always made sure I knew that they were make-believe. A few times, however, his storytelling got carried away, and to calm me down he had to look under the bed to make sure there were no monsters hidden there. Timid as I was, Grandpa always made me feel safe and cared about.

A few years ago, the tables turned. Grandpa had a stroke, and from that time on he was the one who needed to be looked after. Now that he's so handicapped, I can sense that he's kind of scared himself sometimes. So every once in a while, I go into his room, and if he's in the right mood, I tell him bedtime stories. Sometimes I even tell him one he used to tell me. He always smiles, and his eyes look especially happy when I start talking about Big Foot. Grandpa may not be able to walk or talk, but I know he remembers.

Now and then I just sit and talk to him, even though he can't answer. I tell him how he helped me overcome my fears when I was just a little guy and how grateful I am for him now. And whenever I feed him or give him a drink, I always give him a big hug, because he's the one who taught me that it's all right for men to show affection to each other.

My grandfather is the most loving person I've

ever met. I don't think he's going to live much longer, but I hope I've learned enough from him to be just like him. For him, love was the most important thing in the world. And even though he wasn't really my father, he taught me what a father's love is supposed to be like.

M.R.

A father figure is something very hard to find or even define in my life. I've spent about three-quarters of my life without a father, having a strong, wonderful single mother. Throughout my life there have been men who have inspired me, and a few who have even taken the role of being a father figure to me. But none has been more important than my eighth-grade teacher.

I have great respect for Mr. Parkson because our relationship has always been straightforward. He never has told me anything outside the truth, and I trust him completely. For as long as I can remember, teachers have always told me that I had unlimited potential. Mr. Parkson couldn't have agreed more. Thanks to his challenges and inspirational words, I have begun to realize how truthful those words really are. Like any other relationship, we do have our classic confrontations. He always pulls me aside and sets me straight when he believes I need to get focused again.

In light of my never having had a stable father figure in my life, whether or not I'm qualified enough to say who is the best father is not up to me. But I do know that the person I speak of, Mr. Parkson, is a very influential male character in my life. He has never failed me, and I really appreciate his always taking the extra time to look after, not only me, but all of his students. I really value our relationship greatly just like any son would value his relationship with his father. I will always thank Mr. Parkson for his influential role in many young people's lives, but especially for taking the time to be my "interim father."

D.J.—AGE 15

PART TWO

I didn't always have the answers
To every little how and where and why . . .

As dads, we'd like to think we know everything, and when our little boys ask us simple questions, we swell with pride while teaching them godly lessons and helping them learn about life. But we don't always have all the answers. In fact, as fathers, we learn a lot of lessons from our boys. And when we have to learn those lessons the hard way, some of them hurt.

No father is perfect, and most of us would just as soon forget the times when we've done the wrong thing, said the wrong words, or behaved in the wrong way. With God's help, we manage to correct ourselves soon enough to let our sons know about it. And by God's grace, we can receive His forgiveness, ask our sons to forgive us, and—hardest of all—forgive ourselves for our fathering mistakes.

Football was life and breath to me as a young man. I played both high-school and college ball, and there were those who thought I might have a shot at the pros. Even after a knee injury kept me from continuing my participation, I still followed the sport religiously, but I really missed being personally involved.

When I was in my thirties, my first son was born. Dustin was, to the eyes of all concerned, my spitting image. He was huge and healthy, and by the time he was three, it was quite clear that he was athletically coordinated. A new hope dawned in me—football was in my future again!

Dustin played Pop Warner ball until high school, where he was quickly recruited for the varsity team. By the time he was a sophomore he was a six-four tight end and played the position well. As a senior, he received three awards: an all-state scholar-athlete citation, an all-league first-team position, and athlete of the year. I couldn't have been more proud. I never missed a game, pacing the sidelines, yelling at the coaches and refs, and dreaming of a football career for Dustin.

As the recruiting letters began to arrive from universities, I got even more involved by calling coaches and setting up interviews, but I never noticed how unenthusiastic Dustin was. Finally one afternoon he walked into my office and asked if he could talk to me. "Dad, there's something I need to tell you . . . ," he began.

To my astonishment and horror, Dustin informed me that he had never really liked football and that he simply did not want to play at the college level. I looked at him in disbelief. He was the living portrait of an athlete—tall, muscular, and graceful. He was smart and quick and talented. How could he not want to play college ball?

"I know I've got a lot of talent and good size and all that," he explained. "But there's something I don't have and that's the right attitude. I don't like hitting. I don't like being hit. The game is too violent for me. And I want to focus on my studies—how can I do that and commit to the kind of road schedule a Division I team has?"

I argued with him. I cajoled and begged and tried to manipulate him. All the while, my heart was breaking. In my view, Dustin was letting me down. Dustin was rejecting my dream. Dustin was a wimp. Dustin had a problem.

The debate raged for weeks, and I was beside myself with frustration and annoyance. My respect for my son was all but gone, and I felt a real anger toward him. "I never thought I'd be ashamed of Dustin," I told my wife. "But he's got problems."

"No, sweetheart," she quietly answered. "You're the one with the problem."

"What's that supposed to mean?" I snapped.

"I mean you have been trying to live out your dreams through your son instead of letting him live his own life. Dustin is eighteen years old. He's played football for nearly eight years, and he ought to know whether he likes it or not. I hate to be so blunt, but what business is it of yours whether he plays or not?"

35

I stormed out of the house, jumped into the car, and drove—too fast—until I calmed down. After an hour of rage, I gradually realized that my wife was right. My son was a peaceable person without a strong competitive edge. He didn't have an angry bone in his body. He was gentle and kind. Football wasn't his sport—it was mine. I was too old to play, and he couldn't do it for me.

Today my gentle giant of a son has a Ph.D. in history. He teaches and writes, and he has accomplished far more than I. He has no regrets; I have only one. I wish I'd learned to butt out of his life a little sooner. He didn't deserve the kind of criticism he endured from me.

G.D.

My father doesn't mean much to me because he's really never been there for me. Maybe he acts like he cares because he gives me everything I want, but I don't believe him.

A father is someone who helps his child through thick and thin. A father teaches his child how to play sports and gives him love. A real father goes to games and takes his kid out to eat afterward and tells him he played good. A father is there to help his child with his homework.

My father figure isn't anyone, but I can picture the perfect father. He would actually live with me. He would wrestle me out of bed and cook me breakfast. Then he would drive me to school. Then he'd be by my side and love me forever.

P.L.—AGE 12

When my son, Evan, was about five years old, we were on a family outing in the mountains of southern California. Evan and I had visited a mineral and gem exhibit and were amazed by the dazzling multicolored interiors of otherwise earth-brown rocks. I wanted to buy some of them, but Evan was convinced that it was much more important for him and his dad to set out and find these "gems of the earth" on their own instead of paying the buck and a half each for machine-polished marvels of nature.

So off we went, down to the lakeside, armed only with a couple of hammers that happened to be in the trunk of my car. We searched for just the right size rocks to smash. After amassing a virtual pyramid of geological specimens, we set to tapping. We tapped and we smashed and we crumbled and we pulverized every rock we could find. After a while, I sensed the inevitable. There was to be no brightly colored payoff at the center of any of these way-too-ordinary lake rocks.

I stopped for a moment and watched Evan. He was intently tapping away as the sun began to set on the lake, igniting his white hair into a red-orange blaze of color that outshone any gemstone. I admired his stamina. I admired his stubborn diligence. I admired him. As the sun sank on the horizon I was deeply moved, so grateful to God for my son.

I was also grateful to God that, unknown to Evan, I'd had enough sense to purchase secretly a bagful of those beautiful stones from the gem store. Just in case.

B.C.

When we first had our son, I wasn't sure I wanted to have a family. And I was very sure that if we had one child, I didn't want any more. I didn't think I had enough love to go around for both my wife and a child. And I seriously doubted that I could love two children and my wife at the same time. So Brady was our only child.

I'm not sure I was the greatest father in the world, but I must have done something right, because Brady has grown up into a remarkable man. I have learned so much from him that sometimes it feels as if he is the father and I am the child.

Brady and his wife, Linda, have four sons, and every one of those boys is a bright student, a great athlete, and a good citizen. But having four kids just isn't enough for Brady. He and Linda have taken several foster children into their home, and in fact they are in the process of adopting two of them.

One of the important lessons I have learned

40

from my son is that it is possible to love a lot of people at the same time. He wholeheartedly loves every child in his family, spends time with each one, and is aware of their individual needs and problems. He also loves me, and he has proved it to me in a very unique way.

Over the past three years, Brady has taught me to read and write clearly. I was so ashamed of my poor reading skills and had always tried to hide them from him. But he knew, and one day he sat down with me and explained that he thought I had a learning disability. "You aren't stupid, Dad. You just need to learn this stuff differently."

With everything else he has to do, Brady took the time to teach me. Today I can both read and write clearly enough to no longer feel embarrassed. But much more than that, I have learned from Brady a big lesson about love—there's plenty of love to go around, in him and in me and in everybody. All we have to do is give it and we'll get it back.

L.T.

When my daughter, Julie, went out on her first date, I sat her down beforehand, warned her about the predatory nature of young men, cautioned her about the risks of drinking, dancing, and necking, and made sure she had several phone numbers in case she needed a ride home.

When Trevor, my son, went out on his first date, I tossed him the car keys, winked at him, and said, "Good luck."

"What's up with that, Dad?" he said. "Don't I get a lecture like Julie? Aren't you going to give me the same list of dos and don'ts you gave her?"

I laughed and patted him on the back. But Trevor wasn't laughing. He had a very serious look on his face, and he seemed to be genuinely disappointed in me.

My face felt hot. "So what do you want me to tell you? Not to drink and drive? Not to get some girl pregnant? I thought you already knew all that." There was a sarcastic edge to my voice that I didn't like, but I didn't like feeling embarrassed, especially in front of my son.

Trevor studied me for a moment, then turned to leave. "Never mind . . . ," he muttered as he rushed out the door. "We can talk about it later."

I did some serious thinking that evening. I'd heard the talk about women's rights and sexual harassment and the importance of virginity and all the rest of it. But deep inside, until that awkward encounter with my son, I had never really faced up to my own "boys will be boys" attitude. It was the way men thought when I was young, but unfortunately it didn't exactly fit with my Christian beliefs or with my protective feelings for my daughter.

"I need an attitude adjustment," I told myself. "And I need to talk to Trevor."

When we finally sat down and had a conversation, that young man amazed me. He was amiable and relaxed, but he didn't mince words: "Dad, you think like one of those 'good old boys.' You really love God and Mom and Julie, but you're not quite willing to give up your view of women as toys, or whatever it is you guys think."

I stared at him coldly. *A good old boy? Me?* "Trevor, I'm not as far gone as you think. I kid around, but I don't really believe that way."

Trevor shook his head. "Dad, you need to think about your protective feelings for Julie, and then think about the girls I take out. How would you feel if you were their dad? Or look at it this way—would you wish Julie's date 'good luck' and wink at him when they leave the house together?"

I sat quietly for a few moments, fighting off the hot, defensive feelings that surged inside me. Finally, I took a deep breath. "You're right, son. You're right. I need to change, and I'm not too old to change."

Trevor nodded and smiled. "That's good," he said.

From that day on, my relationship with Trevor has been different. Once I stopped trying to impress him by being "one of the guys" and recognized my responsibility to him as a role model and Christian example, I was able to see the whole picture differently.

Not long ago Trevor told me how much it meant to him when I admitted I'd been wrong. "You really blew me away." He grinned. "I'm glad you weren't too proud to admit that you were wrong. It's really helped me own up to my own mistakes."

"Well, we live and learn," I told him, wishing I had learned a few things a little sooner.

H.E.

For years I had poked and prodded Gordon, my oldest son, to be a better student, to get higher grades, to get better scores on his exams. I was always a little disappointed in him because he never quite measured up to my standard of excellence. I knew he wasn't stupid, but I wasn't satisfied with his B-average academic performance. It wasn't that I had been such a great student, it's just that I expected better things from him.

When Gordon was a senior in high school, the student body decided to invite parents to an awards assembly so that we could see our kids honored for their various accomplishments. I was rather puzzled by the invitation. Clearly, Gordon was going to be awarded for something, but I couldn't imagine what.

We received a program when we got inside, and I didn't see any possible award that would fit Gordon. I began to feel annoyed. Had they just invited us to fill seats? I would have to sit there and see every straight-A student marching up the aisle, getting applause, while my son sat in the back of the room. Why didn't he try harder? Why was he so mediocre? My attitude grew steadily worse as the ceremony went on.

By the end, I was fuming. But then the principal went to the microphone and made an announcement: "For the first time this year, I am presenting a special award to a young man who has been so exceptional that we could not overlook his accomplishments . . ."

He called Gordon to the front, and then spent several minutes describing my son's fine character, kindness toward others, trustworthiness, and quiet leadership. "We have never had a student quite like Gordon in our school," he said. "And there may never be another one. So we're giving you, Gordon, the first and possibly the last Principal's Cup award for integrity, diligence, and decency. Thank you for what you've brought to our school. No one who has really gotten to know you will ever be quite the same again."

In that moment, I realized that he was talking to me. I had never really gotten to know my son—much less appreciate him for who he was. And I knew that once I did, I—his father—would never be the same again.

P.R.

Like so many others, I did not have an idyllic relationship with my father while I was growing up. It started with my parents' divorce and went downhill from there, mostly because Dad was not equipped to deal with a broken family. He had a hard time remembering to call us. He didn't always show up when he said he would. He got behind on his child-support payments.

But after many years and much pain, we've reconnected. One day when I was in college, Dad called me unexpectedly at my dorm. I couldn't believe he had even managed to get the number. He asked if he could come and see me, and that was a big deal, too, because I was in a different state. I really didn't think he'd show up, but he did. He didn't spend a lot of time apologizing for the past, he just said I'd been on his mind and he wanted me to know that he was proud of me. And when he left, he gave me one hundred dollars.

We've been in touch ever since. We'll never share a Norman Rockwell relationship, but we are a work in progress. I credit my heavenly Father with giving me the knowledge and freedom of knowing that Dad loved me the best way he could. Perhaps it wasn't always what I had hoped for or even needed, but it was all that he was capable of giving to me. You can only expect a person to do his best, and Dad did that. He's still giving me his best. I hear from him every month or two, and when he's able he sends a little money "to buy yourself something you want." He's never said "I love you" or "I'm sorry for the past" in words, but he's said it in actions. He's trying to remain a part of my life, and that's what matters most.

One thing I'm sure about—I am a better, more loving parent to my own boys as a result of my relationship with my father. When my first son came along, I was so energized to be everything to him my father wasn't able to be with me. I've felt the same way about all three sons. When my wife and I have problems, I fight with all my heart to keep our marriage together. Again, I don't want my boys to be separated from me or from her.

Last Christmas Eve, Dad flew into town and spent Christmas Day with us. He isn't a talkative guy, and there were times when I wondered if he was enjoying himself, but he was there. And when he left, he gave me a pat on the back and gave me the best Christmas present I've ever had. "You've got a fine family, son," he told me, and there were tears in his eyes. "You've been a better father than I ever was, and I'm real proud of you."

J.F.

My father was an angry man, and in his native country it was not unusual for a man to hit his wife. Slapping a woman around was thought to be an appropriate way to keep the family under control. I often saw my father strike my mother, shove her, or shake her. While he was doing this, he would bellow at her, insulting her and calling her names.

As a small boy, I would watch this kind of thing with a terrible ache in my heart. I loved my mother and felt very protective toward her, but I was too young and too small to defend her. The sense of powerlessness I felt was overwhelming, and sometimes I prayed that God would make me like David with Goliath, empowered enough to destroy the evil giant, even though I was little and weak. Most of all I prayed that she would be safe, and although she was mistreated until the day my father died, she was never seriously injured—at least not physically.

Never once did I admire my father's behavior or justify it to myself. It was wrong, I knew it was wrong, and I hated the thought of it. When I got married, I promised myself that I would never do anything abusive or cruel. I would be reasonable, loving, and gentle. I never even told my wife about my father—it made me ashamed of my family, and I just didn't want her to know.

One night I came home from work and found her in the living room talking very quietly to a man I'd never seen before. He left in a rush, and my jealousy and suspicions were stirred up. "Who is he?" I demanded.

"I'll tell you later . . . ," she told me, looking guilty and embarrassed.

"You'll tell me now," I shouted, grabbing her by the shoulders and beginning to shake her. "You're nothing but a . . ." Suddenly, unexpectedly, I heard my father's voice come out of my own mouth. It wasn't my voice, and the words weren't my words. I released my wife from my grasp and recoiled in horror from my sudden rage.

"I'm so sorry," I began, fighting back my tears. "God help me, it's like seeing my father's ghost!"

After we had talked for a while, and I was sure my wife had forgiven me, I asked her—gently and quietly—who the man was.

"He was an encyclopedia salesman," she explained, starting to cry. "I wanted to surprise you, and I told him that if you came home he should just leave and come back later. I was going to give you a set of encyclopedias for Christmas."

Heartsick, I asked her to pray with me. I took her hands in mine and said, "Lord, I repent from this terrible sin. Forgive me for treating my wife so unkindly. And take away from me any evil ways I have learned from my father. I can hardly believe I did what I did, and I don't ever want to do it again. Please take this terrible thing out of me, and don't let it happen again."

Never before in my life had I so clearly understood how much we learn by example. And never had I seen, firsthand, just how powerfully influential a father's example can be.

J.O.

I am fourteen years old, and my father left me before I learned to say "Daddy." Even though my father's not around, in my heart he is always here. Every birthday and every Christmas I cross my fingers in hopes that my father will come home. Does my wish come true? No, but I never quit looking and hoping.

What hurts is seeing other boys with their fathers walking hand in hand or talking and laughing together. I can see how much those dads love their boys, but I can't see my father loving me as his son. See, in my life, there's no daddy to say "good morning" to me. When morning comes, it's just me.

I see my father a lot in my dreams, but never does he turn around. I call for him, but he just keeps walking away. I'd like to believe he misses me, but how can he miss a stranger?

Every time I blow the candles out on my birthday cake, I wish the same wish that I have for the past thirteen years. I wish that stranger would turn around and look at me. Maybe if he saw all the pain and suffering in my eyes from living without him, he would become a part of my life. For now, all I can do is to wish and never give up hope, for hope is all I have to hold on to.

Even though it's hard to say, my father means the world to me, and if I had the chance to tell him all of this, I would not change anything. But I would add a couple of "I love yous."

C.S.—AGE 13

PART THREE

Did I hug enough? Did I care enough?

When you most needed me, was I there enough?

Giving affection and speaking words of approval come easily to some of us but painfully hard to others. It all seems to depend on how our dads treated us. Some dads have to learn new ways and start new traditions, breaking the cycle of aloof or abusive fathering they learned in boyhood.

The more I've read about fathers, the more I've discovered that warmth and affection from dads make a difference in their sons' emotional health, in their view of themselves as males, and in their personalities. Boys who are hugged frequently by their dads even score higher on IQ tests! Travel, work demands, or divorce makes it hard for some fathers to do all they'd like to. Being there for our boys—hugs and homework, fun and finances, play and prayers—may take some effort on our part, but it's the very best legacy we have to offer them.

My little boy, Will, was the most angelic-looking child I had ever seen. When he was around five, he had a round, cherubic face and wide brown eyes. His mother was always cuddling him, talking baby talk to him, treating him like a little prince. My dad hadn't been that way with me, and I was afraid to show him too much affection for fear he would be spoiled or somehow made "girlish." But I loved Will, and I wanted to be closer to him. I just didn't know how.

When he was about five, he was outside riding his big-wheel tricycle when a car driven by a neighbor hit him. Will's head was bashed into the pavement. His mother was there to hold him, call the ambulance, and ride with him to the hospital. I arrived from work, shaken and scared.

At first he seemed to be conscious, but he was not really aware of what was going on around him. He kept asking the same questions over and over. Even when we answered him, he seemed not to hear us and went right back to the same question: "What happened? Did I hit my head or something?"

Will's mother was doing a lot of praying with one of her friends. I was terrified. Will's mind was clearly damaged. Was it temporary or was it something that would trouble him for the rest of his life? My hand shook as I reached out and placed it on top of his. It was the first time I had ever tried to hold his hand. He didn't respond.

The doctors knew Will had suffered a concussion—that much was obvious. But they were concerned about the possibility of a cerebral hemorrhage, so they suggested that he have a CAT scan to check that possibility. When Will was rolled into the big white tube he was not really aware of his surroundings. When he was rolled out, he was back to his usual state of awareness. "Hi, Dad." He smiled. "Where am I?"

"You're at the hospital, Will. You had a pretty bad accident. But you're going to be fine now." By then I was fighting back tears of relief.

He was quiet for a moment, looking around

the emergency room with his big brown eyes. His mother had stepped outside to say good-bye to her friend, who had to get back to work.

"Dad?" Will's voice sounded faraway and very small.

"Yes, son, I'm right here."

"Dad, would you do me a favor?"

"Of course I would. What do you want me to do?"

"I want you to hold me. I'm scared."

I started to tell him that his mother would be right back, but my heart overruled my head. Before I had time to think about it, I sat down beside him and gently put my arms around him. He hung on to me for dear life, and for some reason I started to cry and I couldn't stop.

After a few minutes, Will said something I will never forget. "Dad," he told me, "you need to hug me more often."

I thought about my cold, distant father. About the hour before, during which I wasn't sure if Will would ever be the same. I leaned over and held him again.

"I'll tell you what, Will. How about if I promise to hug you every day until you're all grown up. Would that be a good promise?"

He smiled his huge, angelic smile. "That's good, Dad. And I promise to hug you back."

J.D.

Dad was determined to pay child support. Even though he didn't want the divorce, he made up his mind that he would take care of my brother and me, no matter what it cost him. I can remember thinking it was kind of a big deal for him to have two jobs—one as a mailman and the other as a teacher at a local college.

One fall, the dentist told my mother that I really needed braces for my teeth. I had several really crooked teeth, and my overbite was so bad that he thought it would give me problems with my jaw later on if we didn't get it fixed. Of course Mom had no extra money around, and braces cost about four thousand dollars. She felt bad about it, but she told me it wasn't real likely that I would get braces, at least not for a few years.

One night we were all starving, and Mom was too tired to cook so she called for a pizza. She wrote a check, gave it to me, and went to her room to rest and talk to her boyfriend on the phone.

After about twenty minutes the doorbell rang, and I rushed over to open the door. Who was standing there but Dad, with a pizza box in his hand!

After a couple of seconds of shocked surprise, I said, "Dad, what are you doing here?"

Dad looked a little embarrassed. "Didn't you guys order a pizza?" he asked me.

"Yeah, but I didn't know you were delivering pizzas," I said. "I thought you were working as a teacher at night."

"I am. I work as a teacher on Tuesday and Thursday nights, but I had some free time so I took an extra job."

"Dad, you mean you have three jobs?"

He looked at me thoughtfully, and I could see he was trying to decide what to say. Finally he just shrugged. "I get bored if I don't stay busy."

About a week later, Mom told me we had an appointment with the orthodontist to see about getting braces for me. I was puzzled. "We can't afford braces," I reminded her. "You said it would be a few years . . ."

She shook her head and smiled. "Your father

wants you to have braces as soon as possible, and he says he'll pay for them. It's the *least* he can do," she added bitterly.

I still don't know exactly what caused my parents to get a divorce, although Mom always made it clear that Dad had done something unforgivable. But I do know this—Dad loved my brother and me enough to work around the clock to provide for us. And in all the years we were growing up, we always had everything we needed. He made sure of that.

R.O.

There's nothing exciting or exceptional about my father. He's a plain-looking guy, and I guess he's pretty ordinary in every way. He has worked as a carpenter all his life, ever since he dropped out of high school. He doesn't read well, and his handwriting and spelling are pretty terrible. But my father has the biggest heart of any man I've ever known.

He always wanted to be sure that I was able to take care of things, so when I was four years old, he gave me a toolbox and some of his old tools. From that time on, he never fixed anything around the house or in our neighborhood without taking me with him. We put together my Christmas swing set. We repaired the patio furniture. We fixed a lamp for the widow next door.

First, Dad would patiently, carefully explain what he was doing, and then he'd ask me to help him. Sometimes he had to do things over two or three times, but he never got mad or frustrated. He seemed to know that I would eventually learn. And little by little, I did.

He did the same thing with our pickup. First, he showed me how he checked the oil, then he taught me how to check the oil myself. He explained how to measure the air in the tires, and before long I was checking the air and water by myself. By the time I was twelve years old, I could change the oil and lube the engine without help.

One day when I was fourteen, Dad and I were driving down a country road on our way to my grandma's house. All of a sudden, Dad pulled the truck over to the side and handed me the keys. "It's time for you to learn to drive, son."

I was both excited and scared. I climbed into the driver's seat, put the key in the ignition, and turned it. I'd always watched Dad shift gears, so I thought I knew what to do, but it wasn't as easy as it looked. I stalled the engine three times, finally got rolling, ground the gears into second and third, and then killed the engine again at a stop sign.

I was all over the road, because when I tried

to think about shifting gears, I forgot to look where I was going. It's probably a good thing no one else was on the road, or we might never have made it. But as nerve-racking as it must have been, Dad never once raised his voice. He never got mad or even ruffled. When we pulled into Grandma's driveway, I somehow remembered to put the clutch in and brake at the same time without crashing into the barn. As we came to a stop, he grinned from ear to ear at me. "I knew you could do it. You're going to be a great driver, son."

I've heard it said that parents are supposed to give their kids two things—roots and wings. My dad did both. He made me feel like a part of him, and I always wanted to be where he was. Yet he prepared me to go out into the world by giving me the skills he thought I needed to be a useful and successful man. Today I own my own construction company, and it is named after my dad. He is the reason for my success.

S.S.

Sometimes our boys think they have to be men before their time. Somehow a little boy gets the idea that he has to grow up and act like a man even though he is still a child at heart. Then, when he suddenly feels and acts like a little kid, no one is more surprised than him.

When my corporation moved from Dallas to Nashville, it meant uprooting our children from their schools, friends, and familiar surroundings. Emily, our sixteen-year-old daughter, was the most vocal about her displeasure. She fumed and fussed and cried, and my wife and I spent a lot of time trying to help her make the adjustment as smoothly as possible. Paul, our oldest boy, was already in college, so he wasn't especially concerned.

At twelve, Steve was our youngest, and he never said a word about the move. He stoically packed up his belongings, said good-bye to his buddies, and headed east in the family car. He never looked back.

Once we got to Nashville, the four of us stayed in a hotel for a night, then we went to our new home and waited for the moving van to arrive. I made a fire in the fireplace, and soon we were in the midst of the chaotic process of unloading innumerable boxes and furniture items. The rooms were piled with unopened parcels, people were running around trying to figure out where things went, and we were all feeling seriously disoriented by the time the empty van pulled away.

I had been preoccupied all day, and although I'd made a special effort to be sure that Emily's things were all in her room so she could stay busy putting them away, I hadn't seen Steve for hours. I glanced around the house and finally found him sitting on a box in front of the fireplace, staring vacantly into the cluttered room.

"Steve," I called to him. "What's going on?"

He looked my way and started to answer me. Instead of words, a huge sob erupted from the depths of his heart. Tears poured down his cheeks. When he looked at me, the expression on his face was one of complete humiliation. He had betrayed himself with his unexpected tears, and I could immediately see that he thought he had disappointed me.

I rushed over to him and took him in my arms, where he sobbed for several minutes. "I'm sorry, Dad . . . ," he said.

"Sorry for what, Steve? Why should you be sorry?"

He began to tell me how frightened he was and how lonely he felt. The change was overwhelming; the fear of the unknown was crushing.

Steve had tried so hard to be a little man. I told him how proud I was of him for being so strong and how normal and right his emotions were. At the same time, I told myself how important it was for me to make sure he remained a child as long as he needed to be one.

L.G.

My parents were German immigrants, and they were both strict in their discipline and distant in their relations to their kids. I had to work really hard to overcome my innate discomfort with being affectionate and with expressing my love for my two sons. I especially struggled with relaxing with the kids, laughing with them, and not always retaining a position of authority or superiority. For some reason, it was hard for me to joke around with them, to laugh at their jokes, or to give them a chance to laugh with me.

When my oldest son was about twelve, he and I started to hunt together. We continued to do so until he got married and had a family of his own. As with most sons and fathers, it was a great experience for us, but it gave me an unexpected bonus.

That first year we got up before dawn, crawled out of our warm, dry rooms, and groggily headed out in the family van. We drove for an hour, and when we finally reached our destination, the deer blind was freezing cold, damp, and dark. And as we settled into it, we were both suddenly struck with the absurdity of the situation.

"We have got to be two of the dumbest people on earth," my son said. "Why would anybody leave a warm bed to freeze to death in a place like this? We're really stupid, Dad."

I was half asleep, and his remark caught me off guard. For some reason, as I thought about our miserable situation, I started laughing uncontrollably. And when I started laughing, so did he. Before long the one-liners were flying, and we were nearly hysterical. It struck me, in the midst of it, that my son and I had never really laughed together before.

That was twenty years ago, and looking back on those hunting trips that soon included my other son, I cherish some of the happiest memories of being a father. Between the three of us, there was camaraderie and excitement and mutual success. But the thing I remember best was the laughter. It was fun for them, but for me it broke down that last barrier of distance between us and made us into real friends.

M.W.

For years I was a foster child. Both my parents were in jail, and I went from one family to another. I got mixed up in drugs, in drinking, and in gangs. Before I was in junior high, I'd been kicked out of schools, busted by the cops, and picked up for shoplifting.

In the various foster homes, I was fed and was given a bed and clothes, but I was always just passing through. The people who take in foster kids are usually wonderful people who really want to help, but most of the time they have more on their hands than anyone could really manage very well. So during those years, one family blurred into another. And no matter where I went, no one helped me with my homework, no one talked to me about my feelings or my dreams, no one was there for me to look up to. I had no one to call "Dad."

But now all that has changed.

A year and a half ago, the most compassionate

man I have ever met became yet another foster father. But this time it was different. As usual, I had no place to go. This good man gave me not only a place to go but a place to stay. He not only took me into his home, but he took me into his heart. I was a stranger to him, and a stranger with a past. He made me part of his family and part of himself.

This man has taken me mountain climbing. We have gone to football, baseball, and basketball games. He has sat with me and talked to me during times of emotional hell when I just couldn't get beyond my rage. He has defended me when I was misunderstood, paid for lawyers to deal with my legal problems, and stood up for me when I didn't have the strength to stand up for myself. He has told me enough times that I'm worth something that I'm actually starting to believe it myself.

This man, who just got married a few months ago, is now officially my adopted father. He gave a boy who was ready, willing, and able to die a reason to live and a chance to experience life. I wish everyone knew him and knew what a good example he is. He is a member of Big Brothers, he is an activist for the homeless, and he is an activist for me. And he's given me something I never thought I'd have—he wants me to call him Dad.

R.R.

Four years ago, my mother's painful struggle with breast cancer ended. This marked an extremely challenging and changing time in our lives. My sisters and I were still young and barely knew anything about being responsible. My dad, despite floods of old memories and a mailbox overflowing daily with hospital bills, managed to maintain the household and continue our education in Catholic school. Throughout this time, Dad taught each of us the important skills of cooperation, patience, and organization.

There are times when I look back and say, "I don't know how we made it." We were left in great confusion after my mother's death. She had been the glue that held our family together. Through his tears, my dad took it into his own hands to learn the basics of running a home. He read sewing manuals so he could repair our clothes, learned to remodel the house, and studied books on family relationships so he could learn how to communicate with both me and my sisters. His positive attitude is our family's guiding light.

Food presented a large obstacle to us. Mom had been an excellent cook, but there hadn't been time for my sisters to learn how to follow in her footsteps, and I'd never once turned on the stove or the oven. Dad quickly figured out that we couldn't live on cold cereal and canned goods forever, so he picked up a cookbook and started at square one. Not only did he learn to cook, but he made me learn, too, and in the process made sure I understood that the kitchen wasn't just a place for girls.

Until we left home to pursue our own lives, Dad never dated and never worried about his personal life. Never once did he walk away from his responsibilities. One day I asked him why he was so committed to us. "Because I love you," he explained. But then he went on to tell me something I hadn't known before.

When Dad was twenty-one, his father, who was only fifty, had died of lung cancer. My dad was in college, but he began to go home every weekend. He taught his younger brothers and sisters how to drive, how to take care of the cars, how to handle their checkbooks, and—most important to him—how to live as Christians. He had a little Bible study for them every week, and he led every one of them to Christ.

"It's not the first time I've had to step in," he said with a smile.

During those years, my father told everyone that we kids were the pride and joy of his life and that his dream for us was that we should follow the Lord and prosper and succeed in the world. Not one of us has let him down. How could we?

C.H.

You call your father "Dad" or "Daddy," "Papa" or "Pop"; I call my father "Abba." I call him baker, cooker, cleaner, laundry doer, sweeper, mopper, helper, and shopper, too. My father is the one who makes our lunches and the one who brings our lunches when we forget them. He is the one who takes me to the doctor and picks up the prescriptions from the drugstore, the one who taught me algebra and teaches me every day how to be like him—the teacher, giver, story-teller, kindhearted man.

Your father is the banker, the lawyer, the plumber. My father is the doctor, fixer, tucker-inner, giver of hugs, and wiper of tears. He is the finder of missing shoes and the solver of prob-lems, the judge and mediator, the giver of every-thing: love, patience, guidance, laughter, strength, support, and time.

You want to be a writer, an accountant, an engineer. I want to be like my father. I want to be strong and wise like he is. I want to be kind and honest and sincere like he is. Whether I become an architect or a journalist, I want to be like my Abba.

My father is a magician. He doesn't pull rabbits out of his hat, he pulls hours. He gives us time. After a long day, after making lunches and going to work and driving the carpool, after dropping the clothes off at the cleaners and making dinner, my father listens to my poems and helps my brothers and sisters with homework. My father has time for all of us.

The best thing is that he loves us, and there is nothing better than that.

N.G.—AGE 17

When I was twelve, a very surprising thing happened to me. My dad, who had always seemed distant and remote, unexpectedly asked me to go fishing with him. He was a busy executive, and he was rarely around on weekends. He never approached me to talk, and I never really approached him. We got along all right around the house, and we watched games together, but we had never had a serious conversation unless I was in trouble at school, which had only happened twice.

Dad's invitation came as a surprise. I was caught off guard, but needless to say I was pleased and flattered by his sudden attention.

We packed up our gear and headed for the marina on Saturday. We rented a boat and started out. Once we were settled in a promising spot, Dad began to talk to me. "You know, son, I'm not much of a communicator. I've always had a hard time talking to you kids, probably because my dad never really had much to say to me.

"But I've noticed some things about you lately, and I think it's time we had a talk. So just bear with me, and I'll do my best to tell you what's on my mind. I can see that you are changing from a boy to a man, and that's a good thing. But I think you may also find this to be a confusing time . . ."

Dad proceeded to tell me everything he could think of about the physical and hormonal changes I would be experiencing in the coming years. At times I could see that he was groping for words, but he didn't miss a thing: acne, body odor, and even sexual feelings and changes.

To my amazement, Dad even talked to me about the emotional differences between boys and girls, and some of the things that might happen if I tried to ask a girl out. He talked almost nonstop for over an hour. Finally he said, "I guess that's what I wanted to say. And I want you to know that I'm here if you need to talk to me about anything. Remember, there's nothing too strange or difficult or off the wall for you to ask me."

I sat there with my dad, feeling the movement of the boat and the wind in my hair, wondering if

I was dreaming. Was this the same man I'd always known?

"Dad," I said, "I am so happy to have you talk to me like this. I've always wanted you to talk to me, but I didn't think you'd want to . . ."

He smiled and shook his head. "It's not easy for me. Like I said, my dad never talked to me, so I'm not very good at making small talk with you or, for that matter, with anybody else. But I want to be a good father, and I want you to know I care about you. Will you feel comfortable asking me about things when the time comes? I really want you to."

I knew right then that Dad was my ally, and that whatever happened he would be willing to talk to me. It wasn't his favorite thing to have personal conversations, but the fact that he loved me enough to do it meant the world to me.

I don't remember if we caught any fish that day. What I do remember is finding out, maybe for the first time, that my dad really was my friend. As a matter of fact, he still is.

R.S.

PART FOUR

No matter where you go . . . always know
You can depend on your father's love . . .
Even when my time on earth is through
There still will be a part of me in you . . .

Life brings change, and change brings loss. Sometimes we lose our sons just the way we are supposed to—they grow up, leave home, and begin a new life of their own. Sometimes we lose them tragically, through death or divorce, and it leaves a hole in our hearts that never quite heals. Sometimes a loss takes place in our sons' or stepsons' lives, and it is up to us to fill it. Eventually our sons will lose us because—God willing—they will outlive us.

Saying good-bye is never easy, whether it is only for a few days, for a few weeks, for a few years, or for a lifetime. Fortunately, life's losses always give God the opportunity to offer us new blessings. And, in the midst of change, we discover new opportunities to bless our sons. As fathers, we long to send them on their way with our love as their heritage. That way, no matter what life may bring, they will always have the treasure of their fathers' love stored up in their hearts.

My father is the most important man in my life. He was loving, caring, thoughtful, and cool. He had a lung disease that made it hard to breathe. But that did not stop him. He used to bring my sister and me to the park. He sat at my side while he helped me learn my ABC's and count my 123's. And he taught me to read. He used to call me Bud-Bud. Every school break, when he was not sick, he took our family for a vacation. Even though my dad is dead, I love him very much. He is the best dad that a kid could ever have.

D.C.—AGE 9

Because my parents both worked hard, we had a comfortable life. We lived in a suburban area in a nice house, drove good cars, and enjoyed plenty of food and clothes. There was never a time when we seemed to be pressed for money; at least if we were, I never knew about it.

But Dad hadn't always been financially comfortable. He sometimes talked about hard times during his childhood when there had been nothing to eat but oatmeal, and his large family had eaten it three times a day without milk or sugar. Dad was a big man, and one of the reasons he struggled to keep his weight under control was that he seemed to have a fear that somehow there wouldn't be enough food the next time.

About once a month we had a family ritual that was so much a part of our family life we never even thought about it. I guess I assumed all families did what we did. On a Saturday morning,

Dad, my sister, and I would go to the market and buy apples, oranges, other kinds of fruit, snack bars, crackers, and cheese. We'd carry everything home and put it in two or three dozen plastic bags. Then we'd drive down to the skid row area of the city.

I remember how grimy and sad those streets were. Trash was piled up in the gutters, and men in filthy clothes lay sleeping against the sides of buildings, while other men shuffled aimlessly along the sidewalk. For an hour or two, Dad would pull the car over to the side of the road and hand out the bags of food to the homeless people. He took special care to make sure that the women and children we saw had extra food. And that day, for lunch, we had our own bags of food—we ate what the homeless people ate.

Once we were teenagers, my sister and I began to get a little tired of the routine. We'd have things to do on Saturdays, and we were beginning to feel embarrassed by Dad's obsessive concern for the homeless.

"Son," he told me quietly when I complained

about having to get up early one Saturday morning, "we have so much to be thankful for. We need to keep in mind that other people aren't as well off as we are. That means giving up two things—time and money. And as long as you're living under this roof, you're going to make some small sacrifices so other people can have a few small blessings. Is that asking too much?"

Dad died a year ago. And last Thanksgiving, my wife and children and I went down to a downtown mission and served dinner to the homeless. My kids complained a little, but by the end of the day they were enjoying themselves almost as much as I was.

P.L.

My dad was an alcoholic. Ever since I can remember, I never saw him without a drink in his hand. He divorced my mother while I was still a little boy, and I didn't understand at that age what that meant except that he didn't live with us anymore. From that time on, I didn't see him very often.

As I grew up, Dad spent time with me now and then, but only when it didn't interfere with other plans he had made. He was not at many of my soccer games and did not attend my high-school graduation. He was always too busy. Naturally, it used to hurt me that he didn't enjoy those special moments in my life that meant so much to me.

After high school, I began to carry a grudge against my father. When people talked about "dysfunctional" families, I always made a point of talking about him, his drinking, and his negligence. I guess calling myself an "adult child of an alcoholic" gave me some kind of an identity. It also gave me a bitter spirit toward my father.

Then, about five years ago, my father was told he had cancer. That will change your outlook in a moment. From the time I heard about his illness, I never again thought about all the times we had missed. I only thought about the time we had left. God must have touched my heart in some miraculous way, because in a matter of a few seconds I forgave my dad for everything he'd ever done wrong.

I remember sitting by his bedside and looking at him. His face was so worn and weary; there was so much sadness in his eyes, and yet they seemed to light up whenever I walked into the room. Every visit seemed as if it might be the last. Whenever I kissed him good-bye, I wondered if I would ever see him again. He always said, "Thank you for coming. Thank you so much for looking after me." I knew him well enough to know that he was deeply sincere.

One day he put his hand on mine and said, "Jason, do you know what remorse is?"

"Sure, Dad. I know what the word *remorse* means. It means—"

"No," he interrupted. "I asked if you know what remorse *is*. Because I do. And remorse feels worse than cancer . . ."

On October 20, 1993, he passed away. Although he was never at my soccer games or graduation, he was my dad. I learned to love him, and I love him still. And I know that he is looking down on me today, and he is proud of me.

J.P.

I waited till I was thirty-five to have my first and only child. I waited that long thinking it might help avoid the very situation I find myself in today. My son, Alex, will be four years old in January, and his mother and I have been divorced for two years now. It breaks my heart to see the most important person in my life not have what I was so blessed to have—two parents at home who loved their God, their children, and each other without reservation. My son deserves that . . . all children deserve that.

The day my wife asked me to move out, I sat down with Alex and tried to explain that I was going to be living somewhere else. "Daddy go?" he asked, getting up to go with me. My heart nearly broke. He was too little to understand, but then I wasn't sure I understood either, and I was nearly forty. He reached out for me to pick him up and carry him to the car. "Not this time, buddy," I managed to choke out. "But I'll see you tomorrow."

I moved three blocks away so I could spend every evening with him. His mother asked me to come only on weekends and tried to get a court order to keep me away. Fortunately, my attorney prevailed. It wasn't easy, and it wasn't cheap. But my son still spends time with me seven days a week. And I'm working two jobs to pay for child support and legal fees.

Some of my relatives and friends shake their heads and say, "It isn't worth it. You don't have a life." Is it worth it? There is no question in my mind. I am sincerely thankful every day to God for giving me a handsome, healthy, and brilliant son who is my best friend and loves me unconditionally, just as I love him.

If you met him, you, too, would see that he's wonderful. And I think you'd agree that he's the most precious blessing I've ever received from God.

S.F.

For weeks my wife, Cheryl, sniffled about our oldest son's departure for college. Every time she tried to talk about it, she started to cry and could hardly finish what she wanted to say. I thought she was overreacting, and even though I sympathized with her, I was more than a little condescending in my response to her pain. She tried to explain to me that our family would never be the same and that all the years we'd been together, day after day, would soon be behind us. I heard her words, but they never really sank in.

We lived in California, and Ken had chosen a school in Oregon. Rather than fly him there, I decided that I would drive Ken and his luggage to college and get him settled. Cheryl would stay home with the other kids. As we were getting ready to drive away, she and Ken said their good-byes. She cried a little, and although she didn't completely fall apart, I could still feel the deep pain she was trying to control. *Must be a woman thing*, I told myself.

When we arrived at the school, I had a strange sensation as I looked at the plain walls and the old beds in the dormitory room. We had always tried to make sure our children had nice rooms and comfortable beds. The building was old, ugly, and depressing. How could I leave my boy here?

But the worst was yet to come. When Ken's roommate arrived, the two of them started talking about school and sports and things they needed to figure out—like where the cafeteria was and how often they could eat there. Before long, I was shut out of the conversation. I continued to help put things away, but pretty soon some more boys introduced themselves and made plans to shoot baskets later that day. Naturally, I wasn't invited.

I had rented a rather expensive room at a nearby hotel, assuming that Ken would spend the night there. I had envisioned a nice dinner and an evening spent together, with my offering him sound fatherly advice. But when he got ready to go play basketball with the guys, he turned to me and said, "You about to take off, Dad? Give me a call tomorrow morning. Maybe we can have breakfast together."

I drove away from the campus feeling like my heart had been broken. As I sat alone in the hotel's beautiful dining room, vignettes from his babyhood, school days, and athletic competitions rolled through my mind like flashbacks. By the time I had finished my salad, I had lost my appetite. Waves of grief washed over me, and I fought off the tears.

Not only was I losing my son to his new life, but I felt as if he had rejected me. Tears burned in my eyes, and as I fought them off I headed for the room to call my wife. She seemed to understand my feelings and in her usual gracious way did not remind me of my less-than-sensitive reaction to her own "empty nest" emotions.

I didn't sleep well that night, and by morning I was well aware that my next move was not to advise but to let go. Ken chattered at breakfast about his new friends, the terrible food in the cafeteria, and the academic schedule he'd soon be facing. "Thanks for helping me get settled in, Dad." He smiled as I got ready to drive away. "I'll miss you. Tell Mom I love her." I nodded mutely.

"I love you, too, Dad." When I looked at him, his eyes were brimming with tears. So were mine.

"I love you, son," I managed to choke out, and as I drove away I was crying like a baby.

D.S.

When my wife, Karen, was in her ninth month of carrying twins, the doctors discovered that one of the babies had died in the womb and the other one was seriously at risk. Understandably, our excitement about the birth was replaced with anxiety.

We lived in a rural area, and to my dismay and frustration, when it came time for the delivery, I had to stay home with our other children while Karen was rushed to the hospital in an ambulance. The hospital was several hours away. After a long and difficult labor, our second son was born. He died just minutes after birth.

Meanwhile, I was desperate. For hours, I sat by the phone waiting for it to ring. Finally the call came, but it brought the worst possible news. I asked to talk to my wife, but she was still anesthetized. I was completely alone in my pain. I wrestled with God, infuriated that He was so distant, so silent, so seemingly uncaring. Finally I began to pray, but all I had to say to God were words of bitter anguish, emotional agony, and profound anger.

As the hours passed, I raged aloud, shouting, "Why couldn't I have been there to hold my dying son in my arms? Why were we separated? Why couldn't I have been there with Karen? *Why?*" I carried on like this for a long time.

At last, drained and exhausted, I fell silent. That's when I heard the voice of God speaking quietly—a still and small voice—somewhere in my heart. He said only one thing to me: *I know just how you feel.*

My grieving wasn't over, but for the moment that message of understanding and compassion was enough for me. I knew it had not come from my tortured mind. I knew it was beyond me even to imagine such a tender and gracious response. It didn't bring our babies back. It didn't wipe away all the tears. But it began a process of comfort and healing, a process I was able to pass on to Karen and to the other children.

I never met my twin boys, but I know that they

are waiting for me in heaven. And once I see them there, hold them in my arms, and tell them that I love them, my grieving will be complete.

G.C.

When I was coaching college football, a young boy walked on at the start of the school year, wanting to play on the team. He wasn't a great player, and he didn't bring any awards or impressive statistics, but when I checked with his high-school coach, he said, "He'll work harder than anybody else at practice, and I can promise you that his dad will be at every game. He's one of those inspirational kids, if you know what I mean."

So I put him on the team. And just as his coach had told me, he was a disciplined, faithful team player. He was a defensive back, and in practice he dropped as many balls as he caught, and he didn't always get the plays right. But that committed young man never once missed a practice, and his dad was always in the stands, even though his son rarely got into a game.

One day, while we were getting ready to play at an out-of-state school, the boy got a telegram. I didn't pay much attention at the time, but just before the game he came up to me and told me that his father had died. My heart ached for him when I saw the stricken look on his face. "Don't worry about the game," I said. "You just get yourself back to where you need to be. And don't worry about practice next week."

But on Monday, there he was at practice, working as hard as ever. Afterward he asked if we could talk. "Coach," he began, "this is kind of hard for me to ask you this, but I want you to do me a favor. I want you to let me start the game on Saturday. I know I'm not that great, but it's for my dad . . ."

I nodded and promised to think about it overnight. The truth was, we were facing a very tough opponent on Saturday, and the last thing I wanted to do was play that kid. We needed to be at our best. But something kept nagging at me, telling me to play him anyway. And so I agreed to let him start.

To make a long story short, he tore up the field. He played like an all-American. And when we were down by five in the fourth quarter, he intercepted a pass and ran it all the way back for a touchdown. After the game, which we won by two points, the guys lifted him up on their shoulders and carried him off the field.

Naturally I told him how proud I was. Then I asked him a question that had been very much on my mind. "What motivated you to play like that, when it's the first game your dad hasn't been to?"

"Coach, maybe you didn't know this, but my dad was blind. He's in heaven now, and this is the first game he's ever seen. I just wanted him to see me play my very best."

B.N.

The day I heard that my father was dying, I ran out to the office parking lot and began the twelve-hour drive that would take me to his bedside. I didn't tell anyone where I was going. Instead, I called the office and my wife from my cell phone as I left town, not caring what they would say or what they would think. My mind was completely focused on my father and on the terrible realization that I might never see him alive again.

Miles and hours flew by. I only stopped once to grab coffee and use a men's room. Otherwise, I just kept driving. And as I drove, I remembered. I relived the happy times of childhood when Dad and I were together. My high-school baseball and football games. The movies we saw. The Christmas mornings we shared. Learning to drive. Watching the Super Bowl together. I also recalled the disagreements and the disappointments. Most of all, I remembered his laughter, his big, rough hands, and his kindness to others.

When I got to the hospital, I found Dad barely conscious. I know he recognized me, because he reached out with his big hand—now weak and shaky—and took hold of me. His eyes weren't clear, but they fixed themselves on mine, and I knew he wanted me to know that he was glad to see me. Not long afterward, he slipped into a coma, and he never woke up again.

My mom urged me to go home with her and sleep at the house. The nurses told me that I could sleep in the waiting room. The doctor mentioned a couple of nice hotels nearby and promised to call if there was any change. But I couldn't seem to tear myself away from Dad's hospital room. I just sat on the side of his bed, held his hand, and waited. I waited there all night, listening to him breathe, wondering what would happen next. Sometimes I prayed, and sometimes I just watched. But I could not leave the room for more than a minute or two without feeling irresistibly drawn back.

Early in the morning, just before dawn, I picked up a Bible someone had left in the room, and I began to read from the Gospel of John, chapter 14: "Let not your heart be troubled: ye believe in God, believe also in me. In my Father's house are many mansions: if it were not so, I would have told you. I go to prepare a place for you. And if I go and prepare a place for you, I will come again, and receive you unto myself; that where I am, there ye may be also . . ."

As I read, Dad stirred a little. A nurse in the room at the time touched my arm in excitement. "Look!" she said, pointing to the instruments. "All his vital signs have stabilized. He must be listening!"

After I finished reading, everything remained quiet for nearly an hour. Then, without warning, the instruments sounded an alarm. The room quickly filled with medical personnel, and before I knew what was happening, Dad was gone.

I will always believe that my father went on to his mansion that morning and knew very well where he was going. And I also believe that the same One who came for Dad, to receive him to Himself, will also come for me some day. And when the time comes, Dad will be the first person there to welcome me home.

T.K.

Jim is my stepdad. Even though he is my stepdad, I see him as just my "dad." I've never seen my real dad. I've only known Jim for three years, but I feel like he's been my dad all my life. My dad is there when I go to sleep at night, and he's there when I wake up in the morning. There are times in the morning when he takes me to school and buys me breakfast, too.

My dad teaches me the difference between right and wrong and even punishes me when I do wrong or bad things. I know that even though he gets mad or punishes me, he does it because he loves me.

At night when I am ready for bed, my dad stays with me sometimes twenty or thirty minutes just talking to me about my day at school. He is there for me and gives me advice and makes me laugh a lot. On weekends he takes me to the lake early in the morning, and we play catch.

Everyone who has a stepdad should have one like mine. Just because he isn't my real dad doesn't make him any less a daddy to me. He is very much my dad to me in every way, and I love him very much. I hope I grow up to be just like him. Oh, and he also taught me how to use the computer.

J.T.—AGE 10

From kindergarten through high school, my sister, Caroline, and I attended a very elite private school in our neighborhood. Our classmates came from the finest families in the community, and they all seemed to have one thing in common—substantial wealth. Their mothers were socialites; their fathers were the most successful men in town—doctors, lawyers, investors, and international executives. Some of those dads were gone for long periods of time, and our friends occasionally remarked, "Dad will finally be back next week," or "Dad's going to be living in Europe for a few months."

Caroline and I, on the other hand, saw our father every day. That's because he went to school with us. Our dad worked as the school janitor.

Dad believed in education. He believed in it because it was something he had always lacked. His own father had died when Dad was twelve years old, and Dad had quit school to help support his widowed mother and six brothers and sisters. He didn't read or write especially well, and years later his work as an automobile mechanic brought in only enough money to meet our family's basic needs. So when Dad learned that employees at the private school received a huge discount on their children's tuition, he began to consider a new career path. And when the school learned of his intentions, they told him that we could attend there at no charge as long as he remained employed. That was it—Dad was committed.

He did far more than sweep floors and clean bathrooms. He repaired and tuned up and renovated and restored anything and everything belonging to the school. He answered the phone when the receptionist went to lunch. He helped referee our sporting events. He was a beloved and highly respected member of the school community. Never once in all our years there did we hear a word of criticism or a hint of mocking about our father and his humble, hardworking presence on campus. And when we graduated, Caroline and I were valedictorians of our senior classes. And on both occasions, Dad was in the front row, tears pouring down his weathered cheeks.

Since those school days, Caroline and I have both graduated from fine universities, pursued successful careers, and been blessed with financial security. Dad takes turns living with us in special guest quarters that are reserved especially for him. Our dad taught us to respect him because he had such respect for us and for the intelligence and talent that he saw inside us. He taught us that with hard work, diligence, and a cheerful attitude, anything can happen. I only hope that he is at least half as proud of us as we are of him.

B.C.

PART FIVE

*A promise that's sacred, a promise
from heaven above . . .*

I've heard it again and again. Fathers often say, "I never really understood God's love for me until my son (or daughter) was born." And it's so true—the love we feel for our children, the way we sacrifice to provide for them and to help them, and our desire to see them become their very best are really small versions of our Father's love for us.

We give to our sons because God gives to us. We long for their purity because God longs for our purity. We protect our children because God protects His children. We defend them because God defends us. And we better understand God's willingness to lay down His life for us when we think about what lengths we would go to in order to save our children's lives.

But of all the things we do for them, nothing we have to offer is more important than the gift of faith. The spiritual blessing a father passes on to his son is a powerful and eternal gift. Knowing how precious our sons' lives are to us, I pray we will also remember how essential it is for us to introduce them to their heavenly Father. It is our privilege to guide them into spiritual truth, to teach them the ways of God's wisdom, and to lead them into His loving arms. Only then will we stop trying to do everything for them ourselves and allow Him to love them and care for them as He alone can do.

When I first learned that my wife, Suzanne, was pregnant, I'll have to admit that I had mixed feelings. Naturally I was excited by the idea that we were about to have a child of our own—a baby who would be part of both of us. But I was also scared. I was well aware of the kind of responsibility a baby would bring, and I struggled not to worry about all the things that could go wrong.

The pregnancy flew by, but the ninth month seemed endless to Suzanne, and the doctor was fairly sure our baby was past due. We grew more anxious and were beginning to talk about inducing labor when the big day finally arrived. Early one morning—too early—we headed for the hospital. Suzanne was in quite a bit of pain, and I couldn't drive fast enough to get her there safely. I tried to hide my nervousness, but I'm not sure I succeeded.

Once she was admitted, the time spent in the

delivery room went on longer than either of us had imagined. During the various stages of labor, some of my worst fears intensified. What if the baby wasn't quite normal? What if something happened to Suzanne? What if they both died? During that endless wait, the idea of a real live baby coming into the world was eclipsed by all the medical procedures. But my fears persisted. And as Suzanne's discomfort increased, so did my silent prayers. I don't know when I've ever felt so powerless and so completely dependent on God.

Finally, toward the end of the day, the baby's head crowned, and minutes later, Jason was safe in my arms. I couldn't take my eyes off him. He was perfectly formed, and he was making some surprisingly loud sounds, which left little doubt about the good condition of his lungs and voice. But after the first few moments he settled down, and that's when I really fell in love with him. Because he did something I could never have imagined.

Jason was less than fifteen minutes old, yet he began to respond to the sounds in the room. First he turned his head slightly toward the nurse when she said something to the doctor. Then he turned his head the other way when some instruments were picked up and moved, clattering together noisily. And when I spoke to him, he turned his head again and tried to focus his eyes on my face.

I was moved to tears. This tiny infant, who had not even taken a breath half an hour ago, was already participating in the world around him. He was more than healthy and whole. He was alert. He was responsive. He was a unique and vital human, born into our lives to fulfill some still-unknown destiny. During that almost sacred time, I was overwhelmed with indescribable joy. God had just given to me the greatest gift I could ever receive—a son of my own. My first prayer was to give him back to God.

S.Y.

Daddy was a tough old farmer, and when we were growing up in the early 1900s, he didn't waste a lot of affection on any of us nine kids. On my tenth birthday, I got up in the morning, marched into the kitchen, and announced that I was now ten and "nobody can lick me!"

I guess Daddy took that personally. Without a word he picked me up, carried me under his arm out to the barn, broke the thin sheet of ice on a water trough with my head, and threw me into the freezing cold water. I returned to the house minutes later, shivering and humiliated, knowing who was boss.

But despite his hardness, Daddy cared about the souls of his kids. I lied about my age and enlisted in the navy when I was seventeen. Before I left for basic training, he handed me a New Testament. Patting me a little awkwardly on the shoulder, he quietly told me, "Keep it with you, son. You'll need it. Mom and I will be praying for you."

I nodded my thanks and rushed out the door, glad to be out of the house and on my way.

During the 1920s it wasn't unusual for uniformed sailors to go out on the town with a hotel room key in our pockets. We'd get drunk and pass out, and somebody would see that we got back to our hotel rooms. Normally that's the way I spent my off-duty weekends.

One Friday night, for no particular reason I could ever remember, I wasn't in the mood to drink. I went out to the usual bar, got bored with the whole scene, and went back to my room after a couple of beers. It was a cheap room—just a bed, a dresser, and a toilet. Naturally there was no television in those days, and there was nothing for me to read—nothing except a Gideon Bible.

I had nothing better to do, so I opened it up and turned to the only verse I knew—John 3:16: "For God so loved the world, that he gave his only begotten Son, that whosoever believeth in him should not perish, but have everlasting life."

For some reason, the way the words looked on the page didn't seem quite right to me. I went to my bag, pulled out the New Testament Daddy had given me, and opened it to John 3:16. I looked back and forth, comparing one text with the other.

There was no chair in the room, so I laid the two Bibles on the bed side by side and got down on my knees to study them more carefully. By the time I got up, I realized that God loved *me*. Still on my knees, I asked God's only begotten Son to come into my life.

Daddy's prayers for me were answered. I've walked with the Lord for nearly seventy years now, thanks to his prayers and the Bible he gave me.

K.H.

I think one of the greatest moments in a dad's life happens when his children give their hearts to Jesus. I'm not referring to their acknowledging God because of their parents' teaching. I'm not even referring to those wonderful times of bedside prayer, hearing a precious child's priceless, grammatically disjointed prayers. I'm referring to that one moment when our children, of their own free will and with all their heart, make their own decision to forever belong to Jesus.

I am proud to say that I have witnessed this with both my children. But this is about Evan.

As both a studio singer and a performing artist, I've been involved with any number of musical projects—some more inspiring than others. A few years ago, I was asked to sing on some of the soundtrack recordings for a traveling ministry-musical theater called Toymaker's Dream. I didn't think much of it until months later when my

125

family and I were invited to see their presentation at the Maybee Center in Tulsa. I was moved by how simply and passionately and *loudly* the gospel was explained through this unique presentation. At the end of the musical came a time of response.

My son, who had been glued to the show from the start, grabbed my hand and sweetly said, "I want to go."

Tears welled up in my eyes. I asked him, "Do you know what this means?"

He replied with great confidence, "Yes, Dad, and I want to go."

Throughout Evan's life, I had tried to mirror the love of God to him. And now, at this presentation, somehow it all came together. Suddenly he really understood. He really understood, just as I had done so many years earlier, how intimately and passionately he is loved by the Lord.

I will be forever thankful to the cast of Toymaker's Dream. I am thankful to Evan for his sensitive and responsive spirit. But most of all, I am thankful to the Lord for so faithfully revealing

Himself to my son at a time when I could share
the experience with him.

B.C.

My father is a preacher and a darn good one at that. Although some people complain about being PK's or preachers' kids, I was always proud of my dad. I felt really happy that he was the pastor of our church and that everyone loved him so much. One of my most special memories is that Dad baptized me. Not a lot of children can claim that memory, but for those of us who can, we truly cherish it.

I was about seven years old when I told him that I wanted to be baptized. He nodded his head and asked me to explain what baptism was all about.

"It's about following Jesus," I explained. "When people get saved then they're supposed to get baptized, too. I'm saved and now I want you to baptize me."

I think he was a little suspicious. We'd had a baptism service a week before, and I'd seen all the participants getting hugs and presents afterward.

He wasn't so sure my newfound zeal wasn't a way for me to get lots of attention from the congregation. But after talking to me for a while, he seemed satisfied with my sincerity.

When it came time for those of us who were baptism candidates to go to the changing rooms and put on our white robes, I was shaking all over. I wasn't sure why, but I knew this was a very important time. Still trembling, a few minutes later I stepped into the warm baptistery waters. Dad took my hand, helped me down the stairs, and gently led me to stand next to him.

The organ was playing a hymn I knew called "Where He Leads Me, I Will Follow." I'd heard that song hundreds of times before, but it sounded especially beautiful that night. After asking me a couple of questions, Daddy said, "I now baptize you, Charles Edward Simpson Jr., in the name of the Father and the Son and the Holy Spirit." When he said those words, quite unexpectedly, he began to cry. And the minute I heard his voice break, I started crying, too.

Dad immersed me in the water and lifted me

up again. Then we put our arms around each other, and we just stood there and cried. Everyone in the audience started to applaud. I wouldn't be surprised to learn that the angels were singing. But all I could hear was my dad's voice, "Just as the Father said at Jesus' baptism, 'This is My beloved Son in whom I am well pleased,' I want you to know, Eddie, that you are my beloved son, and I am so pleased and proud of you, too."

I've never forgotten that moment. It felt like both my heavenly Father and my earthly father blessed me at the same time.

C.S.

It's not that my father doesn't love me. I think he just doesn't know how to love. I have never seen him show affection to anyone—not even to my mother. He travels a lot, and when he is home, he's sitting in his chair watching television or reading something.

Dad doesn't like to be interrupted from what he's doing, and when he does talk to me, he always tries to turn every conversation into an argument. I have just had to accept that he is the way he is. I can pray for him and ask God to change his heart, but I've come to realize that I can't make him change. For one thing, he doesn't think he needs to change, and until he does, I guess he won't.

But God saw my need for the kind of fatherly love and affection I'd never known. When I was sixteen, a family that I used to do odd jobs for "adopted" me. Since then I've gotten to experience the kind of family life I'd always dreamed about. I call these people "Mom" and "Dad," and they have filled a huge void in my life.

For a while I thought that I was gay, because I wanted so much to receive love from a man, and I misunderstood my longings. But these good people helped me understand that I wasn't looking for sex but simply seeking the attention and affection I'd never received from my dad. My "adopted" dad never lectured me or tried to change me. He just hugged me, complimented me, listened to me, taught me how to do things, and helped me see the good things in myself. He talked to me about my longings for intimacy and how God had created me to be a man by His perfect design.

Two years ago, I fell in love with a beautiful red-haired woman who stole my heart. The first time I talked to her, I started thinking she was the one for me. And after a few more conversations, I was sure. We were married last summer. She and I are so happy, and we love each other so much I can hardly believe my good fortune. We're now expecting our first child, and I hope it's a boy so I can be the kind of dad I always wanted to have. My parents aren't all that excited about being grandparents. But my "Mom" and "Dad" sure are. And our baby's middle name will be one of theirs, whether it's a boy or a girl. That's my way of saying thank you to the man and woman God chose to be my "other family."

P.D.

Until I was ten years old, I didn't know I was adopted. I grew up in a large Scottish family, and I was the youngest child. As a small boy I had been sickly, and my mother had always seemed to take special care of me, so I imagined that she loved me best. My dad was distant with me, but he was that way with all of us. And the people who came to our home to visit—and there were many of them—always treated me just like they treated everyone else.

There was one man who came, however, who always spent time with me and never seemed interested in anyone else in the family. His name was Nigel, and whenever Nigel arrived, he always brought me a small gift or a candy. My mother would come and find me, and she and Nigel and I would sit in the kitchen and have tea and visit. Then, before he left, he would take me for a walk somewhere.

I never thought much about Nigel's visits. He

was a quiet man and never had much to say to me, and he never offered any information about himself. He just came and went, and of course I was glad for the special attention.

When World War II began, many young men Nigel's age went to fight in France, and one day the word came to us that Nigel had been killed. After she read the telegram, my mother put on the kettle, made a pot of tea, and chased all the other kids out of the house. "I need to talk to Richard," she said.

And that's when I learned who Nigel was.

"When you were born in the maternity hospital, your mom wasn't married. She was a pretty girl with lots of boyfriends, and she wasn't ready to settle down to be a mother. Besides, you were born a month early, and it didn't seem as if you would live. Nigel had been at the hospital, and when he heard that you were unlikely to survive, he carried you here to me to see if I'd look after you until you died. Thanks be to God, you lived."

"But why did Nigel do all that?"

"Nigel was your father, Richard. And he loved

you very much and wanted to be sure you were all right."

"But he never married my mother?"

"She wouldn't marry him. She wasn't ready to be a wife or a mother."

"Where is she now?"

"I don't know where she is. But I know where Nigel is. He's with Jesus, and he'll be looking after you from heaven. Nigel will be praying for you every day of your life. You can be sure of that."

R.N.

My wife and I both attended Christian colleges, and we took a variety of Bible and doctrine courses. We often enjoyed debating various doctrines and beliefs. We were both from Protestant traditions that practiced believers' baptism. But when our first child was born, the topic of baptism ceased to be academic and suddenly became very real to us.

Despite our upbringing and our religious backgrounds, Sandi and I both had a strong desire to see our newborn son baptized as an infant. This was not a difficult decision for us—we were completely in agreement. But it wasn't such an easy issue for our parents. My father in particular was adamantly opposed to the idea. He had a rather narrow view of Christianity, and it most certainly did not include Catholic, Episcopal, or Orthodox beliefs.

The more we talked about it, the more angry Dad became. He bombarded me with every argument I'd ever heard and a few I couldn't have imagined. He stridently opposed our decision and accused us of everything from ignorance to heresy. Fortunately Mom and Sandi's parents, although they also disagreed with us, were not so angry. And when the day of the baptism rolled around, it's a tribute to their love that all four of them were there, sitting in the front of the church.

The young Episcopal priest who officiated over the service was a friend of mine, and he understood our desire to plant a seed of faith in our young son's heart. He shared with us the belief that the Holy Spirit would nurture that seed until Brandon was old enough to understand God's love for him and to obey His call. After we recited the baptismal liturgy, the priest baptized the baby and anointed him with oil. Then he lifted him high in the air, offering his new life to God.

In that moment, as I watched, I felt a deep stirring in my spirit. I almost expected to see a shaft of sunlight illuminate the baby, receiving him into God's family. I glanced at my own father, and I could see that he, too, had been touched by the sight of the uplifted child. I took Sandi's hand and squeezed it. We had done the right thing. The seed had been planted. And by God's grace, it has continued to grow.

B.I.

Being a preacher's kid wasn't easy for me, and when my boys were born, I was determined that they would have as normal a life as possible. I made up my mind that we would always do things together, we would have fun together, and we wouldn't be "religious" all the time or worry about what other people thought. My two sons and I were always great friends, so at least I started out on the right foot.

But when they were around six and eight years old, my church began to grow. Now that was a good thing, but as it grew larger, I became busier. We had services three times on Sundays, prayer meeting on Wednesdays, Bible study on Thursdays, and visitation on Saturdays. In between I had to attend board meetings, trustee meetings, elder board meetings, and appointments with people who needed to talk to me.

I tried to take the boys with me whenever I could, and they often fell asleep on my office couch waiting for me to finish up some late-night conversation. I'd move each one of them to the car, laying one in the back and one in the front seat. Once we got home, I'd carry them up the stairs to their rooms and tuck them in bed. Usually they never woke up until morning.

But one night my oldest boy, T.R., called out to me as I tiptoed away from his room, "Daddy, will you pray with me?"

I turned back and knelt by the side of his bed. First I prayed for him and asked God to give him a good night's sleep. Then it was his turn.

"Lord Jesus," he said in a very sleepy voice, "thank you for my daddy, and for all the things he does for You and for other people. But could You help him spend more time with us? He's working so hard that he doesn't have time for me and my brother. And we need him, too. Please help him to make it to my baseball game on Saturday . . ."

I hadn't known there was a game.

". . . and help him to come to open house at school next week . . ."

I hadn't known about that, either.

". . . and help Mommy get some rest because she's really tired. Thank You, Lord. In Jesus' name, Amen."

After he was finished, I said, "Son, you never told me you had a game Saturday."

"I have a game every Saturday, but you've got to visit people so I didn't tell you."

"I'll be there, buddy. And I'll be at open house, too."

Sobered and saddened, I went into the living room where my wife had fallen asleep reading a book. I told her what had happened. She nodded and smiled. "You've got a lot to do, honey, and we don't want to distract you from God's work."

"God's work?" I cried. "What is more important to God than my family? If I can't take care of my family right, how can I help the rest of the people in the church?"

I asked Sharon to forgive me for my negligence. And I promised her that I'd talk to the elders the next day about how I could spend more time with her and the boys. Then she and I prayed together.

That evening's conversation led to the hiring of the most wonderful assistant pastor I've ever met. He's done more for our church than I could ever have done on my own, and he has worked with me now for nearly twenty years. It all began with my little boy's prayer. It touched my heart almost as quickly as it reached God's heart. And its answer has blessed every person in our family and our church and has even made a positive difference in our community.

W.B.

The Lord bless thee, and keep thee: The Lord make his face shine upon thee, and be gracious unto thee: The Lord lift up his countenance upon thee, and give thee peace." This passage, found in the Old Testament book of Numbers (6:24–26) is sometimes called the Aaronic blessing. One of the things I learned as a Christian father was to bless my children with it.

I always tried to take the time to bless them when I prayed with each of them at night, and sometimes I also blessed them when I said good-bye to them. I would lay my hand on their fore-heads and speak the words quietly. I wanted it to mean something special to them—something like "Daddy loves you, he's not mad at you for any-thing, and he's praying for you." The blessing became almost automatic, and sometimes I won-dered if it meant anything to the children. I knew God would honor it, but the kids and I never really talked about it. Did they even notice what I was doing?

When they were still in elementary school, my job involved a lot of travel and I was always on the go. One day at the office I received word that I needed to catch an afternoon flight. I rushed home and hurriedly packed a suitcase. Just as I was pulling out of the driveway, my youngest son walked up on his way home from school. I hurriedly rolled down the window and said, "I'll see you tomorrow night. I've got to go to Atlanta."

He nodded and smiled. "See you tomorrow." Then without another word, he stuck his head in the window. I can still see him there, as if it were just yesterday, bowing his head and closing his eyes, waiting for me to bless him.

G.K.

When my son Scott called and asked to talk to me, I didn't want to take the call. My wife, our other children, and I had been through years of ups and downs with him and his drug abuse. We'd heard a thousand promises and seen them broken twice as many times. Scott had stolen from us, manipulated us, and failed us. He had broken my wife's heart and turned my optimism into cynicism. It had been a relief not to hear from him for two years. Now he was on the phone, and he was just about the last person on earth I wanted to hear from.

"Get his number and tell him I'll call him back," I told my secretary, wanting time to think. When I saw the area code, I realized that Scott was in a different state, and my curiosity was stirred. When I finally got myself psyched up to place the call, I was surprised when the woman who answered said, "Oakridge Christian Center."

"Could I speak to Scott Granger, please?"

"Who's calling?"

"His father, returning his call." There was a brief pause, and then I heard Scott's voice.

"Hi, Dad. Thanks for calling me back . . ."

So began the most amazing phone conversation I've ever had. Scott told me that he had been through another rehab program a year and a half ago but this one had provided something no other program had offered. "I met Jesus Christ," he explained.

"What does that mean?" I asked, wondering if he'd really lost his mind this time.

"It means that I've been forgiven for my past, that Jesus died for all my sins, and that He's given me a new life. And I want to ask you and Mom to forgive me, too. I'm born again, Dad. I'm a new man."

He went on to tell me that he was actually working for the church, helping other addicts get their lives straightened out. I was speechless, torn between the hope that he was really straightened out this time, fearful that he had become some kind of a religious fanatic, and

147

cynical with the cold, bitter thought, *Right. Here we go again.*

The young man who arrived at the airport two weeks later looked like a stranger to me. He was well groomed and nicely dressed, and his eyes were bright and clear. He was probably as nervous as I was, but he quickly and spontaneously took his mother in his arms, and they both began to cry. I was braced for deception, but there was an undeniable difference in this initial meeting.

In the days that followed, Scott told us his story. In the midst of drug withdrawal, he had seen a vision of Jesus Christ on the cross and had cried out to Him for help. His withdrawal symptoms had ended instantly, and the experience had led him to a church. "I asked Jesus to be my Lord," he quietly explained. "And my life has never been the same since."

My wife and I had never really been church-goers, but the change in Scott was too dramatic to ignore. And when he showed us the story in the New Testament about the prodigal son, we discovered that just as we had welcomed Scott home,

God was waiting with open arms to welcome us home, too. Today, ten years later, our family is a Christian family. Jesus has taught us about forgiveness, new life, and renewed hope. He has given us back the son we had lost.

And He has given us the same new life He gave to our prodigal son.

J.G.

My father was a redneck who made a point of wearing a crew cut when all the hippies were growing their hair long. He had a good-sized tattoo on his right arm from his days as a sailor in World War II. And he didn't like sissies.

I had always tried to be strong around Daddy. He wasn't a mean man, and even though he would cuff me occasionally for back talk or failing to obey, he let me know he loved me by spending time with me, playing ball with me, and praising me for doing well. But I never saw my father cry, and I never saw him show any sign of emotional vulnerability.

Daddy taught an adult Sunday school class when I was growing up, and I never heard him teach. But one year when we had our junior-high camp in the mountains, somebody asked him to speak to our youth group. I was uncomfortable with the whole thing. Parents are pretty embarrassing when you're thirteen, and I was fairly sure Daddy had no idea about the way kids thought or the things we cared about.

When he got up to talk, he asked everyone to turn in their Bibles to the story of Jesus' death on the cross. He explained—very well, I thought—about the cruelty of crucifixion, the terrible pain it caused, and the humiliation and shame of a Roman cross. He was better informed and more articulate than I had expected.

Then something happened that I will never forget. Daddy began to explain that Jesus had not died as a victim or been forced to the cross by a mob but He had died by choice. "He came to die," Dad said. "He came to earth to die for you, and He came to earth to die for me. Because of my sins . . ."

Suddenly his voice broke. He tried to continue, and he could not. He pulled a handkerchief out of his pocket and wiped his eyes. After a deep breath, he started again. But as soon as he tried to describe the love Jesus has for each of us and to explain the reason He had gone to the cross, he was too choked with emotion to go on.

Finally, Dad said, "I'm sorry. I can't finish the story. All I can say is, after what Jesus did to save you, don't you want to give Him your life? If you do, come and talk to me after we're finished." I stared at him in disbelief and felt hot tears burning my eyes, too.

The room was utterly silent. For a few minutes not a person stirred or whispered or, it seemed, even breathed. We sang a quiet chorus, "Thank You, Lord, for saving my soul . . ." And the next thing I knew nearly half the kids in the group were standing around my father, talking to him and praying with him. Without a second thought, I got up and joined them.

L.H.

One evening, when I was about six or seven years old, my dad told me it was time to go to bed. So off to bed I went. Dad was always the one who would kneel down with me and help me say my prayers. But that night I had a question. For some reason I had begun to wonder, *Does Jesus really hear me when I pray?* I couldn't believe that the God of the universe who made heaven and earth would take the time to hear a curly haired, freckled-faced little boy pray.

I finally found the courage to ask, "Daddy, does Jesus really hear me when I pray?"

My dad's eyes were full of love when he answered.

"Are you serious, buddy? Jesus *waits* for you to pray. He counts the minutes and even the seconds. It is one of the highlights of His day, just like it's the highlight of my day when I come home and get to spend time with you. So, you had better hurry up."

153

With excitement pounding in my heart, I almost shouted, "Okay! Then I'll make it a good one!"

Dad never failed to let me know that he loved me more than anything in this whole world, but he also made sure I knew that Jesus loves me even more. Of course God's love is unexplainable, but I really believe that a father's love here on earth is a taste of what we will feel some day when we stand before our heavenly Father.

R.H.

We're here for fathers!

National Center for Fathering

P.O. Box 413888

Kansas City, MO 64141

1-800-593-DADS

E-mail: dads@fathers.com

http://www.fathers.com

_____

_____

_____

_____

_____

_____

_____

_____

_____

_____

_____

_____

_____

_____

_____

_____

_____

_____

_____

_____

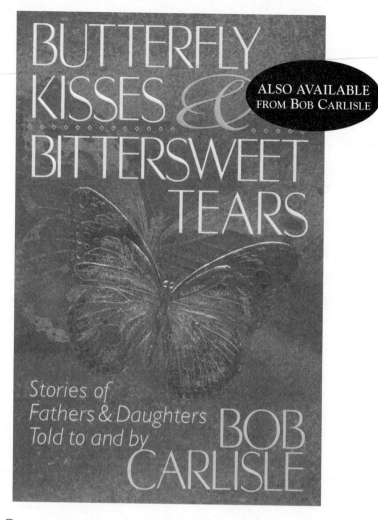

ALSO AVAILABLE
FROM BOB CARLISLE

BUTTERFLY
KISSES &
BITTERSWEET
TEARS

*Stories of
Fathers & Daughters
Told to and by* BOB
CARLISLE

STORIES THAT BIND DADS AND DAUGHTERS
TOGETHER FOR A LIFETIME

Bob Carlisle topped *Billboard's* national charts with his hit song
"Butterfly Kisses." This touching collection inspired by Carlisle's song is
one that every woman will want to give her father and
every dad will want to share with his daughter.

WORD PUBLISHING

Available at Bookstores Everywhere.